HOW TO PROTECT YOUR FAMILY IN TODAY'S WORLD

A hands-on, practical guide to protection strategies

H. Stephen Peckron

authorHOUSE™

1663 LIBERTY DRIVE, SUITE 200
BLOOMINGTON, INDIANA 47403
(800) 839-8640
WWW.AUTHORHOUSE.COM

First published by AuthorHouse 08/31/04

ISBN: 1-4184-9276-0 (e)
ISBN: 1-4184-9275-2 (sc)

Library of Congress Control Number: 2004096926

Printed in the United States of America
Bloomington, Indiana

This book is printed on acid-free paper.

Table of Contents

<u>Preface</u>

How many times have you heard the expression "if only I had known …?" Well this book's mission is to provide you with an ongoing basis for protecting you and yours from the rest of the world in the most conceivable risk areas. To be aware of life's risks and how to protect oneself from them is something rarely taught in school. Most will tell you that many times it is learned the "hard way".

By the careful reading and re-reading of this practical guide you should be able to avoid many of life's misfortunes. You and your family will benefit from this hands-on practical guide to protection tools and techniques.

In it you will learn financial, health, national disaster, terrorist, career, insurance, and other personal items of interest impacting your family. Along with specific ways to eliminate or reduce these risks are websites and other source materials that allow you to go further if you wish. Risk is an evitable part of life. How you respond to it, by ensuring you and your family's security is up to you. This book is your guide.

I.
Introduction: Nature of Risk In Today's World

This book deals with risk protection for you and your family. Whether you are single, a hybrid family, the traditional family or other type of relationship, this book can save you countless hours of grief. All you need do is to identify a perceived risk that threatens you in your current environment – financial, career, medical, etc. and apply the tools suggested.

Some of you may not be aware of the many risks that are present in today's world. Naturally, only the predominant risks facing most persons will be discussed. Foolish type of risks which a person chooses to assume, e.g., driving while intoxicated, fixing an electrical fixture with the power on, diving into a shallow pool, having unprotected sex with a new partner, etc. are all examples of risks that most rational persons will seek to avoid. These latter risks are expressly ignored in this book.

So let us begin with a clear understanding of what "risk" means to a rational person. Risk is the possibility of loss or injury. This means that something (or possibly someone) creates a hazard which exposes you to danger. The kind of danger to you or your family runs the gamut from financial ruin to physical injury. To put it in legal terms, it's the hazard, danger, peril, exposure to loss, injury, disadvantage or destruction and comprises all elements of danger.

I am oft reminded of General Douglas MacArthur's famous saying that the only certainty in life is uncertainty. This is the basis of all risk – uncertainty in any undertaking – whether it be economic, moral or physical.

Life is fraught with this uncertainty. From our first breath to our last, there are no guarantees. To believe so is a delusion. And at times there appears to be no basis for making any sense of life's vagaries. Why will a cigar-a-day smoker live to his 90's while the nonsmoking marathoner dies in his 40's? Why will the conscientious employee be passed over for an external hire? Why will one car be involved in an accident while another narrowly escapes?

To this mix of life's imponderables is "today's world". Most recognize that the world of the 21st century has far greater uncertainty and risk then the world of the past 50 years. People who study history and note dramatic changes call radical shifts in the world's condition by the fancy phrase of "paradigm shifts". An easy way to identify a paradigm shift is that the change will dramatically alter the level of risk and your future in this world. Here are some examples of paradigm shifts:

- •Industrial revolution

- •Invention of the telephone

- •New world order after WWII

- •Mass production technologies

- •Invention of the transistor

- •Invention of the personal computer and the internet

- •Terrorist attack on 9-11

- •Financial implosion after Enron and other companies

After each of the preceding, individual lives were dramatically affected. The invention of the internet and personal computers altered forever the economic outlook of many occupations by creating new jobs, e.g., systems network analyst and destroying others, e.g. bookkeepers.

What is ironic is that most of the world shifts that exposed persons to new risks could be foreseen. Even the terrorist attack of 9-11 was suggested in a planning scenario but never taken seriously.

To protect ourselves and our loved ones it is vital to seek out these potential risks in the environment, i.e., capture them and decide how to respond. In other words, how can a protective tool or technique be used to shelter us from the perceived or potential risk?

This book is divided into individual chapters with each chapter identifying the specific risks and the protections that eliminate or reduce it. Most beneficial use of the book is by reading it cover to cover. However, if there is a pressing need or risk, e.g., career choice, business, potential hospitalization, then reviewing the Table of Contents for that risk will be a more selective use. In either case, it should be a guide for the future.

II.
Financial Risks

From the moment we take our first breath we become a financial and economic statistic. Insurance companies predict our death and disability. Government views our consumption and savings patterns. Education, housing and advertising record the progress we make throughout our lives.

In a nutshell, aside from being a financial statistic, our human lives have, for better or worse, a financial life. The risk that every person has in their financial life is twofold. At one end is the risk of not having enough financial resources to provide for the basics: food, shelter, and clothing. At the other end is the financial risk that once the basic needs are satisfied, investments must then yield sufficient resources to carry us through old age.

Perhaps one can better identify these two extremes and how they threaten one's financial solvency by viewing the typical life span of an individual in the following table:

<u>Years</u>	<u>Activity – Financial Life</u>

0 – 25   Much of this time is generally spent in school getting an education. Financial solvency becomes a challenge unless parents support the young student into the college years. Even with such support, it is likely that many individuals will emerge from this period of their financial life with educational debt. Some may be already married, in which case the issue of debt becomes most important in their lives.

25 - 35   Graduate school or getting established in a job or career highlights this period. While school is important, it is in this decade that most individuals begin to "find themselves" and their financial lives follow upon that decision. And for those geared to graduate or professional school, e.g., business, law, medicine, etc. the educational debt can be staggering. Of course, it is here that many choose to marry and start a family – a further financial challenge.

35 – 50   The "break-point" in many careers, whether in corporations or professions is the magic number of age 50. Companies downsize, partnerships dissolve,and many individuals question their continued existence in a given career. So this 15 year period is a "coming of age". The financial life has generally(though not always) improved. Children are grown and hopefully departed from the nest to begin their life's journey. With added resources, many individuals have the added flexibility of "trying something different". Once again, financial resources may suffer in this career transition.

50 – 65	The fastest growing segment in the population in the 2000 census according to the U. S.Census Bureau were centarians (those at age 100).Because of advances in drugs and medical science people are living longer. So the 65 "normal" retirement age is a fading concept. Even the Social Security Administration has pushed back the age for full retirement benefit qualification (see www.ssa.gov).These 16 years pose a wake-up call to many individuals. Since most persons are employees, the only resource available is the money saved during their preceding work life. Unlike the business owner who also saved money for retirement and has the added feature of selling an asset or business to cushion retirement, the employee is usually faced with greater financial risks.
65 – 100	This 35 year period is shortened or lengthened by one's individual genes and medical science. But physical life aside, financial life is really what is threatened. In this "final phase" resources dwindle causing some individuals to seek employment. Not a very rosy outlook.

What the above life span table indicates is that financial life can be threatened with a multitude of risks throughout. Some of the more prevalent financial risks follow in the table below:

Years

0 – 25	Poor education; career with no opportunities or low pay; disability or death; excessive debt from student loans or ineffective money management.

25 – 35	Heavy career education debt; ineffective money management; disability or death; career changes; marriage, children and potential accompanying financial risks, e.g., divorce, child support, poor investment management, including education funds for children, care for elderly parents.
35 – 50	Increased medical costs; health risks; ineffective money and investment management, including retirement funds; downsized or departed professions; marital adjustments, e.g., new spouse, retirement planning with spouse, etc., disability or death, care of elderly parents.
50 – 65	Potentially devastating medical problems (e.g. cancer); health risks; ineffective money and investment management, including retirement funds; marital adjustments, disability or death.
65 – 100	Practically certain increased medical costs; substantial health risks; ineffective money and investment management, including retirement funds; disability or death.

When one reviews the prevalent risks throughout the life span of an individual it becomes apparent that some risks are systemic in that they encompass the entire life span while others are more age centric. For example, disability or death is a risk over one's entire life span whereas care for elderly parents generally affects the 35-50 life years in most cases.

The type of protection selected is based upon the actual or perceived financial risk and whether it is a systemic or age centric risk. So let's classify each risk from the table above and identify the kind of protection available to eliminate or minimize it.

Financial Risk

System Risk (6)

- Disability
- Death
- Poor money management
- Poor investment management
- Medical costs
- Health

Age Centric Risks (10)

- Poor education
- Poor career/job choice
- Education debt
- Career changes
- Marriage
- Children
- Divorce
- Child education fund
- Elder care
- Retirement fund

Once these risks are identified the protections one should consider are as follows:

A. Systemic Risks:

1. Disability: There is a statistically greater chance of becoming disabled than dying over one's early and middle years. Yet, many individuals have no protection or opt out of a disability protection in corporate plans on the assumption that it "won't happen to them". This risk can be substantially minimized by purchasing a disability income policy from a reputable insurance company. Hence, protection is available and should be considered even if one is single because it ensures that all or a portion of one's income will be provided during the period of disability.

Temporary versus permanent disability should be considered when the policy is obtained. Also, the Social Security Administration does provide payments in the event of disability.

> CAUTION: How the Term "disability" is defined in the policy is crucial. For example, Christopher Reeve, the actor, is a quadriplegic which is defined in most disability policies as total disability. However, there are policies that would classify the quadriplegic's disability as a partial disability if that person can be gainfully employed. For instance, the renowned British physicist, Stephen Hawking, is a tenured faculty member who continues to teach but is a quadriplegic.

To find more information on disability insurance see www.a.m.best.com and www.ssa.gov.

2. Death: Every living being faces this risk. And the life insurance industry has responded with a myriad array of products: term, permanent, annuities with an insurance wrapper, etc. Is this risk one that can be protected? Of course. But is this risk one that should be protected? It depends.

Most purposes of life insurance are to provide a financial cushion for the decedent's survivors and pay any taxes upon death. But if no heirs exist and no significant tax liability is present and the surviving spouse or partner has substantial assets, then life insurance makes little sense.

> CAUTION: Because of the varieties and features of life insurance it is strongly recommended that a competent life insurance salesperson be consulted, e.g., one holding the credential CLU (Chartered Life Underwriter), should be sought. See. www.a.m.best.com.

<u>3. Poor Money Management:</u> In 2004, a review of public high schools across the country will disclose that few offer a required course for students in economics or money management. Considering that the majority of high school graduates do not obtain a college degree, this lack of economic education is evident.

The basis of budgeting, money management, and other tools are lost on many Americans. While computer tools do make it easier to track expenditures and budgets (see, for example, the computer software package by "Quicken"), the <u>understanding</u> of budgets and money management occurs only with some basic knowledge.

This is a substantial financial risk because it can result in poorly achieving any of life's financial goals: buying a house or car, saving for a child's education, or saving for retirement.

> <u>CAUTION:</u> Many wrongly assume that the more one makes in income, the more they can spend. It is not how much one earns that controls the financial ship. It is how much one saves. Here are some examples.

- A married couple, both physicians, earned well over $400,000 per year but had saved <u>less</u> than another couple, both teachers, who earned about $50,000 per year.

- Mortgage companies and banks are now offering a 125 percent loan. This means that the buyer has no equity in the property and has financially leveraged (borrowed) <u>more</u> than the property's appraised value. If the real estate values go south, foreclosure becomes imminent.

- Certain state 529 college plans for college tuition are not guaranteed by state law. This means, as has happened in some states, that the college tuition plan has gone broke.

There are many ways to increase your knowledge of budgeting and money management other than sitting in a classroom. See www. B&N.com for a listing of basic books that will help you. Also on the web are free courses on money management – use the search engine: www.askjeeves.com or www.momma.com to locate ones that will help you.

> CAUTION: Avoid "debt counseling" firms that guarantee they can get you out of debt. Use only reputable financial counselors that generally charge low or no fees, e.g., not-for-profit.

Here, then, is a risk that can be practically eliminated among the financial risks by just obtaining the necessary tools via books or the web.

4. Poor investment management: Don't confuse the financial risk of poor money management with poor investment management. Investment management means managing your investments. While most consider their home as their principal investment it really is not. You would not usually trade or sell your home on purely an investment basis because of the strong emotional ties. So investments, traditionally rental real estate, stocks, bonds, CDs, etc. need to be managed to maximize their rate of return.

To protect oneself from this financial risk, one must consider that more of the investment one keeps (principal and earnings), the greater will be the investment accumulation. So a rule of thumb to remember in investment management is this: pay no commissions and little, if any, tax on the investment. Every time a commission or tax is paid, the investment's yield goes down – you lose money. This is part of effective investment management.

> CAUTION: Most Americans have a
> 401(k), private/public company plan, 403(b),
> not-for-profit plan, or 457, government plan,
> which allows them to direct their investments.
> If one must choose between a "load" mutual
> fund that charges commissions and a "no
> load" mutual fund with no commissions, the
> latter is typically better. And the long-term
> performance of the load versus no-load funds
> are practically the same according to industry
> studies.

To eliminate or minimize poor investment management, like money management, education is the key and the same suggestions and web sites apply. Do not turn over your investments to one person. Use such persons as advisors only.

> CAUTION: In most states a "financial
> planner" or "investment advisor" can simply
> hang out a shingle. Only deal with Certified
> Financial Planners or such other credentialed
> individuals that charge a flat fee for their
> services – never a commission on the products
> recommended to you.

5. Medical Costs: As anyone elderly or retired will tell you, the real threat to their future financial well being is rising medical costs.

> CAUTION: Many   retirees   from
> corporations take a retirement package that
> includes medical coverage if they accept early
> retirement. This is part of the epidemic in
> corporate America known as "downsizing".
> What the employer fails to tell the early

retiree is that such medical benefits (unlike pension benefits) are <u>not</u> guaranteed either as to the retiree's out-of-pocket cost or even the continuation of the plan itself! I have had many clients over the years who were shocked when their out-of-pocket medical premium cost tripled and others who were informed that their coverage was cancelled.

How to protect oneself from rising medical costs? There are the costs associated with doctor, hospital and prescription drugs. While a confusing new federal government prescription drug plan is available in 2004, most Americans still have substantial risk despite Medicare and Medicaid once they become eligible. Here is one means to help minimize this risk. Obtain Medi-Gap policies and, upon retirement, be certain that practically all fixed expenses are eliminated or substantially reduced in your budget. A fixed expense is one that must be paid usually on a monthly basis where you have little control over deciding whether to pay it or not. Examples would be rent, mortgage payments, car payments, Internet access, telephone service, etc.

Another means of protecting oneself from rising medical costs other than common-sense solutions such as preventive health check-ups (physicals), proper diet, exercise (preferably aerobic), etc. is to use financial and real estate assets to accommodate the increases.

Techniques such as the reverse mortgage (when the retiree's home mortgage is fully paid), increasing the investment earnings distribution as to the increased medical costs, and purchasing long-term care policies will be a useful means to minimizing this financial risk.

<u>6. Health:</u> Much of the preceding concern over rising drug costs and medical costs can be reduced if one monitors their own health. So the systemic life decision is simple. Take charge and be responsible for your own health.

Think of your health as a precious gift, much like your eyesight. The human body, as physicians will tell you, is rather amazing. It will begin to remedy a harmful injury or behavior once it's stopped. Thus, when one stops smoking the body begins to repair the internal damage caused by it. There are preventive "fixes" to tip the odds in your favor that, while not a guarantee of health, will reduce the likelihood of ill-health. Here are the "shields against ill-health" that you should consider immediately.

<u>Shields Against Ill- Health</u>

<u>Shield No. 1: Diet</u>

The old saw that "you are what you eat" has never been more true. Atkins diet aside, eat intelligently for yourself. The math is simple. If you consume more calories than you burn in a day you have a net <u>positive</u> caloric intake. You want a balanced (as to lose weight) or <u>negative</u> caloric intake. But understand that even this rule can change with circumstances. A pregnant woman, the long-distance runner or marathoner, the person coming out of the hospital or from an illness, all probably require a positive caloric intake. Eating a plant-based diet, low in sugar and saturated fats is applauded by most dieticians. Go to <u>www.B&N.com</u> and review the many good books on proper diet and nutrition. Also view the many websites on diet by using a search engine, e.g., <u>www.askjeeves.com</u> or <u>www.momma.com</u>.

<u>Shield No. 2: Exercise</u>

Some still believe in Santa Claus and the Easter Bunny. I suggest these same people believe in diet pill claims that weight loss is possible <u>without</u> exercise.

Exercise, which need not be the heart-pounding, red-faced type, is essential for proper weight management and psychological balance. Practically any sound exercise will do – preferably a mixture of aerobic (constant motion like walking, running, or swimming) and anaerobic (start and stop motion like tennis) -- walking at a brisk pace and moderate weight lifting is ideal.

One must also recognize that certain "exercise" regimens called exercise by society are really no exercise for the body. Consider

- Golf: This can be a good exercise if the player walks the course carrying his own clubs. The famous actor, Jackie Gleason, an inveterate golfer, usually consumed a large quantity of Jack Daniels as he rode in a golf cart. He was known to have remarked that "golf is the only sport where he gains weight".

- Bowling: Rarely do most bowlers break a sweat. An easy way to decide if the activity is exercise or just a fun pastime is whether you're sweating. Many bowlers drink beer and eat while bowling and here's another little hint: it's probably not exercise if you can eat and drink alcohol while you're doing it.

- Archery: Another great activity, even an Olympic sport, is archery. Yet, it is not serious exercise because one largely stands still while doing it. You would gain more in exercise by walking 18 holes on a golf course than practicing on an archery range for the same amount of time.

Shield No. 3: Know Thyself

To maintain one's health it is essential to follow the advice of the ages: "Know thyself". Listen to your body. Many times busy people try to "catch up" on physical activity on the weekends and become what is called a "weekend warrior". This is ignoring your body and knowing your physical limits.

Former President Bush on his 80th birthday jumped from a plane and parachuted to the ground. He demonstrates how good health can serve you. But an inexperienced, first-time parachutist in fair health at age 50 may discover that such an activity will result in a broken leg (or worse).

To know thyself the data you collect on yourself and monitor is crucial. Here are the ways to protect yourself from the risk of <u>not</u> knowing yourself:

- Annual physicals: A good annual physical is essential. It should usually involve (depending on one's age and doctor's advice) a physical examination, blood work (chemical blood composition), urinalysis, PSA for males over a certain age or at a higher risk of prostrate cancer, resting EKG, chest x-ray, pulmonary function, comprehensive eye exam, hearing test, and conference with your doctor.

- Body numbers: Ask a woman her dress size and she immediately responds. Ask a man his shirt size and he will rattle it off. But ask either one their BMI (body mass index) and they haven't a clue. As a matter of health protection and to guard against the risk of heart disease, diabetes, stroke, etc., there are certain "body numbers" you should know just like other body measurements.

Body numbers of blood pressure, resting pulse, HDL (good cholesterol), LDL (bad cholesterol) and others need be known. But the BMI number is of particular concern. It is a number that considers a person's weight and height to determine that person's total body fat. The formula for BMI is:

$$\frac{\text{Weight in Pounds}}{\text{(Height in inches) x (Height in inches)}} \quad X \quad 703$$

For example, a 220 pound 6'3" male has a BMI of 27.5. (220/75 x 75) X 703 = .03911 x 703 = 27.495. Is this good or bad? Well the National Institute of Health lists the following as the BMI categories:

<u>You are:</u>   <u>if your BMI is:</u>

Underweight	less than 18.5
Normal weight	18.5 to 24.9
Overweight	5 to 29.9
Obese	30 or more

> <u>CAUTION:</u> If you have a muscular build, your BMI may be overestimated. On the other hand, if you are elderly or have lost muscle mass your BMI may be underestimated.

For simple BMI tables that can be downloaded and (hopefully) placed on the wall above your bathroom scale, see any of the following: www.cdc.gov www.dietician.com; www.wvda.org. Know thyself begins with your BMI.

Shield No. 4: Reduce Stress

This is a big-time silent killer. While some stress is actually good for a person, too much stress is like an electrical short-circuit in our brain. Protective measures to reduce – and some have actually almost eliminated stress – would be the following:

- Learn to have some quiet time. This can be anything from soaking in a tub once the children are down or meditation.

- Simplify, simplify, simplify. Got fifteen IRA accounts? Got a schedule from hell? Got an abusive relationship? Then, today, begin anew. Carpe Diem! Seize the day! You'll be amazed at how simplification reduces stress.

- Exercise, exercise, exercise. No not with the goal of adding more stress but of relieving stress. The British have a concept of "constitutionals" (brief walks) generally after dinner. This relieves the day's stress and let's you smell the roses.

- Watch comedies. Humor helps to pick up the spirit.
  Even in hospitals, patients who watch films of the Marx
  Brothers or the Three Stooges have improved according
  to a study. Humor is the escape value on the pressure
  cooker called life.

- Attitude adjustment. Recent studies reflect the fact that
  one with a positive view of a situation will experience less
  stress in a situation than one with a negative view. After
  all, as the sage tells us "attitude is everything".

- Question the source. If you find that stress is increasing,
  question where it comes from.

A friend once told me that she was getting "stressed out" by
driving in traffic during rush hour. Solution? She moved closer to
her job and now spends the free time riding a bicycle in her new
neighborhood.

Shield No. 5: Control the vices

Alcohol, tobacco and other such vices must be controlled if you
want to shield yourself from ill-health. As Plato said "all things in
moderation ...." This is good advice to this day.

Vices come in many forms. Physical, psychological, emotional,
etc. and need to be identified as such. Take Marie's case. She is
a single mom in a professional career. At dinner she would have
an occasional glass of wine. Her firm downsized and Marie found
herself without a job and two small children. The infrequent glass
of wine became a bottle of wine a day fostered by her growing
depression.

Can vices kill? You bet. And not just the health but, as in Marie's
case, the person's spirit. Fortunately, Marie was smart enough to
surround herself with caring friends who helped her during this
difficult time. Today her health is excellent, her children happy and
she found a position in her field — all by recognizing the damage
that excessive vices can do to a life.

Shield No. 6:   Develop a moral compass

The persons who seem to be the healthiest, when stricken with a loss of health, manage to come through the trial. Why is that? An ideal protective device to guard against the inevitable ill-health as one ages is a strong moral compass.

Just what is a moral compass? It is a person's character in a nutshell.   Aspects include self-discipline, compassion, duty, friendship, industry, courage, consistency, perseverance, integrity, loyalty and faith. These virtuous traits, espoused by many writers and religious leaders, combine together into a human personality that must face all manner of life's difficulties.

Losing one's job can be viewed as frightening or empowering. As negative or positive. As a predicted failure or an anticipated re-birth. But one thing such adversity will do. It will test your mettle. Never lose sight of your moral compass. It will guide you past the turbulent waters to the safety of the shore.

Shield No. 7:   Swim with the current

Anyone who has swam in the ocean knows about rip currents. These are currents that can result in one's drowning if they are fought. So how do you save yourself if caught in a rip current? Swim parallel to the shore until you can break free, i.e., when conditions are optimal.

Of course, to the novice swimmer this is all too rational. Instead, they fight the current and generally lose. Health is a lot like currents. One day everything is fine. The next day you feel a suspicious lump. Hypochondriacs always fight the current and make themselves sick. Positive rational persons swim with the current until they are capable of defeating the ill-health. Many times a person is his or her worst enemy – an enemy, if you will, of the soul.

Prevention teaches us that the systemic risk of ill-health will occur sometime during our lifetime, generally as we age. Why, pray tell, would a rational person seek to hasten it along?

B. Age Centric

1. Poor Education: Today inadequate education can be overcome by job training and adult education opportunities. But pity the poor individual who honestly believes that education is a waste. For that person there is no protection whatever from the risk of eventual economic failure and unemployment.

Understand that education can be formal (as in a school setting) or informal (as on the job training). Regardless of its label, the risk of being poorly educated raises the risk toward a life of crime, poverty and unfortunate consequences.

It is important, therefore, to recognize the following:

> • In the early years: Most formal education occurs in the early years. Here an inadequate public school system may be partially to blame but the young fledgling needs strong wings to fly against the winds of life.

> • In the middle years: Even highly educated and experienced persons may find their skills obsolete. Bookkeepers are a good example. With inexpensive software programs, the two year community college graduate who worked as a bookkeeper needs to upgrade his or her skills by perhaps finishing college or eventually sitting for the CPA exam.

How to prevent this from happening?   Either get a sound education at the beginning or improve an inferior education through some of the many programs available. For example, several top-flight universities now have undergraduate and graduate programs on line. This makes the so-called brick and mortar college a thing of the past. Now practically anyone anywhere in the world can attend a "virtual" (on-line) classroom at an accredited college.

2. Poor Career/Job Choice: Another age centric risk that usually arises in the middle years is the selection of a poor career or job choice in one's early years. I'm sure that buggy whip apprentices believed they had a lifelong occupation. Similarly bookkeepers in the 1950's believed much the same.

So how does one minimize this risk? Protection is not as difficult as it seems. One need only look at the trends. The Department of Labor publishes an Occupational Outlook which can be obtained on-line at www.dol.gov. Occupations in demand in the future are predominated by medical and computer careers.

Also, schools and professional counselors may be of help as will be numerous books written on the subject available at the library or the local bookstore. Selection of a poor career or job can be remedied provided one selects a career or job that will furnish them opportunities lacking in the original choice.

3. Education Debt: In the early years (usually by the mid-30s) substantial education debt for undergraduate, graduate and professional schools may be incurred. Any economist worth his or her salt will tell you that in life the greatest return on investment over time is from education. Not necessarily formal education but education nonetheless.

So it generally does make sense to incur such early costs. For instance, a young person attending a private law school may spend $80,000 for the education. A young physician even more. However, once in practice such professionals will be capable of earning these costs back several fold over the years.

To protect against the incurrence of substantial education debt the following should be considered:

• Use a Section 529 tuition or savings plan. These are special IRS-approved plans that practically all states have for college and postgraduate education. See www. savingforcollege.com for a listing of such state plans.

CAUTION: Some state 529 tuition plans are not guaranteed by state law. This means that they run the risk of financial insolvency. Always ask if the state plan is guaranteed – most are. Also, state tuition plans are run by the state governments or their financial agents. So your control over the money invested is minimal. In college savings plans, you have greater control over your funds because these are run like mutual funds. So be careful in which 529 plan – college tuition or college savings – is best in your situation.

- Consider alternatives to student loans. Colleges have work-study programs (see, e.g., Northeastern University in Boston as an excellent work study school), student federal and state grants (a grant is not a loan) and, of course, academic and athletic scholarships. Never overlook scholarships that are aimed at a particular group or for a particular purpose, e.g., the Fulbright scholarships, scholarships to benefit African Americans, Asian Americans, etc.

- Consider consolidations. If you graduate with substantial educational loans, the National Student Loan Association has information on consolidating the student loans at a lower interest rate or delaying the payment. There are even programs, known as loan forgiveness, that can eliminate or significantly reduce the educational loan.

CAUTION: It is unfortunate when students do not repay their loans. Such educational loans are not discharged in bankruptcy and any future tax refunds will be paid to the Federal agency owed the educational loan.

<u>4. Career Changes:</u> Another age centric risk is when one voluntarily or involuntarily changes careers. A career change can be thrust upon you. Early retirement, downsizing, career obsolescence, etc. are all reasons for this condition.

How does one protect oneself from the threat of a career change? By examining the situation. In other words, embrace the career change as inevitable. It is not uncommon for a person to have several careers in one lifetime. For instance, the late Mary Kay of May Kay Cosmetics built a multimillion dollar business <u>after</u> her career as a homemaker. So did many others.

With longevity increasing, it is likely that more seniors will be pursuing different careers as well. Since the likelihood of a career change is very high, here are the protections one should consider:

- • Make allied changes: It is far easier to go from an R.N. in a hospital to an R.N. in an in-home nursing assistant than to a software engineer. An allied change is a career change to a closely related field within the existing profession or job. A plant electrician changes careers because of downsizing to a residential electrician. Different licensing requirements but same general field.

Such allied changes save time and money. Little additional schooling is generally required and the change, many times, can be accomplished without any significant job hiatus.

- • Consider radical change: Martha just got a divorce. She was a tenured law professor but her children are fully grown and she wants to make a "fresh break". So she is moving to a new city and pursuing a job in journalism.

She doesn't mind "starting over" in a new career in her mid-40's. For Martha it's exciting and provides her a degree of closure on her past life. So new beginnings are good and sometimes they entail a new career as well. But protect yourself by planning ahead for your capabilities and the job opportunities at your present skill, education and experience levels.

<u>5. Marriage:</u>   At some point most persons consider marriage. The risks inherent in marriage are not the same as two single persons merely cohabiting. Why?

Because the law views them differently. Once legally married, certain significant economic and financial risks arise. Indeed, in community property states, e.g., Arizona, California, Idaho, Louisiana, Nevada, New Mexico, Texas, Washington, and Wisconsin, the act of marriage vests one-half of the marital property in the spouse during the marriage. How to protect yourself in the marital situation involves the following:

- Ozzie and Harriet are dead. The model of the husband as the sole breadwinner with the wife as the homemaker is practically dead. Today, the economic realities are such that both partners work and, if not, at least the homemaker works from home or part-time. This means that financial risks are greater since the higher costs of living demand both salaries.

As a precautionary device, disability insurance and life insurance may prove advisable. Also, sound money and investment management should be part of the marriage from day one. Perhaps the easiest way to view a marriage in financial terms is as a true partnership for life. Such an arrangement means that significant financial decisions, as in any partnership, are <u>joint</u> decisions.

- Plan before marriage: If there are substantial assets that one spouse brings into the marriage, then a prenuptial agreement should be made. This is an agreement that covers such things as the claim to the assets upon divorce, nature of the assets and their source, etc. It will protect the partner with the larger assets in the event of a divorce.

- Consider wills and other documents: A last will and testament is necessary unless you have little property (under $10,000) or no heirs or children. Today, it is generally wise to have a will because without one the state where you reside will have a state law that disposes of your property commonly referred to as "intestacy". Consult a good lawyer for these matters and find one by contacting your state or local bar association or go to http://www.findlaw.com.

6. Children: Inherent in the joy of having children are the many risks they will suffer. Risks of ill-health, accident, poor education, and civil or criminal problems are just a few of the predominant ones.

What protections against these risks are available? In large measure, these can be insured risks (unless a precondition excludes the coverage). There are, however, risks that carry no insurance. So an inferior school district which will render your child less likely to achieve the college of your dreams is one such risk. As outlined, through all the various risks, each child is unique, so analyze the risk and then review the materials in this book for protection from that risk.

For instance, if your school district is becoming inferior in your mind because of local budgeting problems (e.g. teachers buy their own classroom materials for the children), then the risk of an inferior education increases. How to protect your child from this risk is based on you – the parents – ability to respond and the priority you place on the risk.

So to protect against this risk you could move to a better school district, send your child to a private school, home school (if allowed in your state), tutor-assistance, etc. Perhaps a combination of protections might be considered. This is the format in solving the risk: protection problems that will inevitably arise with your child.

7. Divorce: While approximately 50 percent of all marriages end in divorce, this is an age centric risk. In the early years of marriage (first five) and the later years of marriage (once the children are grown), the sociologists tell us the risk increases.

How to protect against divorce? It is not as difficult as it seems. If one views marriage as a partnership, the critical feature of any partnership is communication. Hopes, dreams, problems, concerns, etc. all should be communicated to the other partner. Issues of fidelity, religion, raising children, etc. need to be discussed instead of using the "ostrich" approach, i.e., ignore it and it will go away.

Generally, there are no panacea or cure-all protections for the many risks that will arise during the course of a marriage. But if either partner is abusive, addicted to something (or someone), or involved in illicit activity (remember Carmella Soprano – the psychologist told her to end the relationship but the economic cost proved to be too great), then run – don't walk – to a psychologist or family counselor.

Is divorce ever justified? It depends. When the risk to the marital partner is so great that harm continues and no protection from harm (apart from calling the police) exists, then most would argue that divorce is necessary. However, like with the matter of children, the risk perceived by a spouse can be reduced or eliminated through communication and reaching a common ground. Consult the web browser, e.g., www.momma.com or www.askjeeves.com for a listing of licensed family therapists in your area.

8. Child Education Fund: To educate a child can be a substantial drain on the family finances. The prayers that Junior or Matilda will be Rhodes scholars or the next state champion are usually pipe dreams. In order to reduce the risk of not having sufficient economic resources for your child's education there is a protection known as a "529 Plan".

These are IRS-approved plans administered by your state. They come in two tax-advantaged flavors. One is for tuition – a guarantee that the future tuition increases will be covered in the plan. The other is more like a college savings plan where a large amount can be stashed away and managed for your child's education.

Because these plans are so diverse (even within one state) you will want to consult the website http://savingforcollege.com.

> CAUTION: There are other alternatives to 529 Plans. You could, when Junior comes home after his birth, rush down to the local bank and open an education IRA (known as a Coverdell IRA) or open a Uniform Gift To Minors Act (UGMA) (UTMA in some states) account. With UGMA accounts, the minor has an unrestricted right to the funds usually at age 18 (majority age). The lack of parental control over the funds concerns some parents.

Similarly, you can set up a minor's 2503(c) trust. This is far more expensive than a 529 Plan, UGMA or Coverdell IRA. Consult the IRS website for free booklets on the education plans and their tax benefits. See http://www.IRS.gov. And, of course, always consider a good book on the matter at http://www.B&N.com.

9.   Elder Care: America is getting older and living longer. This means that many "baby boomers" will need elder care and the costs, many times, will be borne by their adult children (with families of their own).

How to protect against this risk? Consider the purchase for oneself of an elder care policy issued by a reputable company. See the A.M. Best website for a listing of insurance companies that sell elder care packages and see the Consumer Reports and AARP websites for discussions.

Costs vary dramatically based upon the buyer's age, health, exclusions, etc. so it is probably wise to assist the elderly parents in this decision. And the parents may want to involve the adult children since an inferior policy will cast the economic burden on the children.

Aside from protection via insurance, the selection of the elder care facility or nursing home is crucial. When the parent cannot live alone because of the increased risk of harm, then selection of an elder care facility is warranted. Once again, the AARP website is beneficial.

10. <u>Retirement Fund:</u> The increased cost of living will mandate that many seniors will continue working well past so-called retirement age. This is not entirely a bad idea. In addition to the economic advantages come the psychological benefits of remaining active in a productive way.

There are generally two significant risks in life: dying too soon and living too long. In the case of dying too soon, the young family is left without economic resources. In the case of living too long the person finds that he or she has outlived their economic resources and now must subsist on the government dole or (worse yet) on the largess of their already financially strapped children.

Building a retirement fund and living off of a retirement fund present two very different risks. One builds a retirement fund throughout their working life – assuming that this fund is not disseminated by stock market reversals. Here there is a wealth of information on how to build and manage a retirement fund, e.g., a 401(k), 403(b) or 457 plan. Check out Fidelity Investments and AARP websites along with the many good books written on the subject.

So let's assume that you have accumulated your nest egg of $2 million in savings and that you are 65. It is likely that you may live to 100. So how do you mete out $2 million over 35 years – and still pass on something to the grandchildren?

Far easier said than done. First, the rate that you take distributions is an inherent risk of outliving the nest egg if that rate is too large. Most financial planners and other experts place the distribution rate at 4-5 percent per year. So on a $2 million dollar nest egg this works out to $80,000 to $100,000 per year. Of course, if the interest rates drop (and most retirees use fixed investments like bonds) so does the income.

How to protect against the ravages of inflation, investment losses and poor financial planning? Here are some tried-and-true protections:

- Continue working as long as possible. Not only does this ensure less is distributed from the retirement fund but also that you will remain active. After all, there is just so much golf one can play!

- Reduce all fixed expenses. A fixed expense in a budget is one that must be paid, e.g., rent or mortgage payment, car payment, insurance payment. Most retirees will substantially reduce such payments leaving only variable expenses – which they control. For instance, dining out is a variable expense entirely within the retiree's control.

- Do not place all the retirement fund assets in fixed (bond) investments. Fixed investments by their very nature are interest sensitive and poor hedges against inflation. A good retirement fund is protected from these risks by a portion in blue-chip mutual fund stocks.

- Never place all your assets with a financial advisor. While there are excellent financial planners, trust advisors (the Bush family uses one of the oldest trust companies, Northern Trust), and others, never give up your right to make the ultimate or final decisions about how your retirement fund is to be invested.

- Keep all fees and taxes to a minimum. Every time your retirement fund pays a commission, administrative fee or Uncle Sam, the assets are less for you. How to protect yourself is use the IRA minimum distribution rules once you reach age 70-1/2, use tax deferred accounts, avoid premature distributions (before age 59-1/2), loads (commissions) and in mutual funds find the lowest 12 b-1 fees (administrative fees). See the http://www.morningstar.com website for a listing of such mutual funds fees and pay particular attention to the Vanguard family of funds – one of the lowest 12 b-1 fees in the industry. Also consult the Kiplinger Money Magazine at the local bookstore.

- Distributions should be at 4 – 5 percent per year from the retirement fund. It is a proven fact that most Americans are woefully short at retirement time. So if the savings amount to $200,000 instead of $2 million, then a 5 percent distribution means an annual amount of only $10,000 – below the poverty line. What protection is then available? Aside from the obvious delay of retirement, consider a reverse mortgage that will supplement the $10,000. Again, books and websites exist on the types of reverse mortgages, costs, etc. Be aware, however, that when one passes, the house is now owned by the insurance company that provided the lifetime annuity to the retiree.

- Consider moving to a lower cost state or country. Florida is called "heaven's waiting room" because of the large number of retirees. Not only is the cost of living substantially lower than in the "snow belt" states but Florida is with a handful of states that have no income tax and, in most cases, no estate tax. So many retirees opt for a state that will make their retirement dollars go further. Other retirees go one step more. They shop around for a lowest cost retirement haven in a foreign country. Today you will see American "communities" in Mexico, Belize, Ireland, etc. which feature far lower housing and living costs than in the U.S.

> CAUTION: While one's social security payments follow them, Medicare does not. Consult the website http://www.ssa.gov. for the rules if you are contemplating moving to a foreign country. See also http://www. InternationalLiving.com.

III.
Tax Risks

One of the major risks to a person or family, aside from death, is taxes. This risk – which can follow us <u>beyond</u> the grave – needs to be understood and reduced with the protections discussed below.

A. Tax System: Regular, AMT and Death

In the United States, we have <u>two</u> Federal income tax systems. One is called the regular tax. This is what practically every taxpayer is aware of and requires that a Form 1040 (or some variation) be filed on or before April 15th of the year following the end of the tax year. So 2004 tax year ends December 31, 2004 and 2004 taxes are reported on or before April 15, 2005.

The alternative minimum tax or AMT is known as the stealth tax because it "sneaks up" on millions of Americans. Created to penalize wealthy individuals and corporations, the AMT, since its inception in the 1970's, has become a major problem for most Americans. Unlike the regular tax with rates from 10 to 35 percent, the AMT has only two rates 26 and 28 percent. According to a recent study by 2010 the number of American taxpayer households that will be subject to the AMT will be as high as 35.6 million (this is up from 1.3 million in 2000). The AMT risk is clearly increasing.

Finally, aside from the Federal income tax is the risk of the Federal gift and estate taxes. Gift taxes are ordinarily paid while you are alive, once a year, and the estate taxes are paid at your death. Very few Americans (about ½ of 1%) pay any Federal estate taxes and while more pay Federal gift taxes, the exemptions and other transfer devices, tend to make this a tax largely avoided by most Americans. So as a risk factor, Federal estate and gift taxes do not present the same challenges as the Federal income tax. But the taxpayer's goal should be to minimize all three taxes. That is, don't reduce the income tax liability at the expense of raising your estate and gift tax liabilities. Consult a competent tax advisor, tax CPA or tax attorney for protective measures and, of course, read the many books and consult the IRS website for recent developments.

B. How To Avoid An Audit

Most Americans report their taxes to the IRS and pay their taxes. However, on occasion, you may receive a letter from the IRS on past taxes requesting information and adjusting your prior taxes upward (with likely interest and penalties).

How to protect oneself from an audit? Consider whether you are within a "targeted" group. Common sense dictates, because of limited IRS resources, that not all taxpayers have the same risk of audit. Generally, self-employed, independent contractors (e.g. insurance and real estate salespersons), businesses that rely on cash primarily and other types (a recent IRS target has been taxpayers who invest in so-called off shore tax shelters) are within high priority audit areas.

If you fall in any of the above, e.g., you operate a home business as a self-employed taxpayer, then your risk for audit arguably goes up. But even if not, consider the following audit protections:

- Be certain that W-2s, 1099's, and other tax documents you receive (and the IRS) match and are correct. Audits usually arise by IRS computer. The IRS computer matches documents it receives with what you report on your tax forms 1040 or the AMT 6251.

• Even if you don't fill out the forms (you use a CPA), review and check the tax form. No one is perfect. Even CPA's make errors, so always check the form.

> CAUTION: Some people are under the misapprehension that using a CPA or lawyer to fill out their tax forms takes them of the hook. The case of Leona Helmsley, the NY hotel owner, illustrates this fact. She argued that since the CPA allowed her to deduct certain expenses on her tax form, the CPA should be liable not her. The Court didn't buy it and poor Leona went away to Federal prison for tax evasion.

• Maintain good tax records. Keep bank records, expenses, charge card bills, etc. backing up your return for at least six years. While three years is the so-called limitations period for the IRS to question your return (three years from the due date: 2004 return due April 15, 2005 means that the IRS has until April 15, 2008 to question your 2004 tax return), the six year period is for substantial omission of income (more than 25 percent of your gross income). If you feel the six year period could never apply, then dump the records – never a copy of your return – after three years.

> CAUTION: In cases of non filers, or intentional tax fraud, like murder, there is no limitations period. And real estate records should be kept at least ten years and many argue indefinitely because so many tax problems can arise with real estate (residence, but more so with investment properties).

- Don't commingle business and personal bank accounts. If you have a business account pay only business expenses and record only business receipts. Don't treat it as just another bank account. This is what Leona Helmsley had done in large measure. So if you want to pay for that spa treatment from your business account, have it charged to the business loan account (which you should repay) or, better yet, for your personal drawing account for personal items. Anyone who wants to see additional protections from audit should go to the IRS website (http://www.irs. gov) or pick up one of the many books on the subject, since one taxpayer's situation can be entirely different from another.

C.   Why Not All Tax Advisors Are The Same

Tax advising, like any profession – medical, legal, ministry – has its share of exceptional to dullards. So how do you select a competent, yet financially reasonable, tax advisor?

If you are a large business or wealthy individual, you will consider a large accounting firm. But the rest of us need some protection from the risk of getting the incompetent or worse yet, the unethical tax advisor. Here are some protections to hopefully eliminate that risk as merely reducing it could result in a poor advisor, a risk not worth assuming.

- Only consider tax professionals: The CPA or lawyer who do not prepare their own taxes is probably the wrong long-term tax advisor for you. A tax CPA or tax lawyer may cost more than a general practitioner but they are worth it in the long haul. Can your G. P. doctor set a broken leg? Of course. Should an orthopedic surgeon consult in more serious breaks? You bet. Will it cost more? Probably. But it is your leg we are talking about. So it is with your taxes. Even a well-intentioned G.P. can cost you thousands in tax deficiencies, penalties and interest. Don't accept this risk.

- Always ask for client names: A good tax advisor will be more than willing to give you a listing of several clients that you can contact for reference. Ask if they were ever dissatisfied and how it was resolved. Stay away from tax advisors who refuse this request.

- Watch out for "tax preparers": A tax preparer, bless their souls, is exactly that – he or she will prepare your taxes – not advise you. A tax advisor will be able to consult with you, prepare or have prepared your taxes based on this consultation, and stand ready to assist if ever audited. There are numerous local and national tax preparation outfits. Be wary.

- Don't over-rely on educational credentials—experience is best: The "accredited" or "board certified" tax advisor may be someone only a few years out of school. Incidentally, while the typical CPA has a tax course in college and is tested on tax on the CPA exam, the typical lawyer (nationally) is rarely required to take a tax course and most state bar exams never test on tax! Ask the prospective tax advisor if they ever worked for the IRS before private practice. There is something to be said for the experience gained inside the IRS that other practitioners can only wonder about. Find out how many years they have worked exclusively in Federal (not State) income tax and the kind of tax clients. So if your advisor has worked the past 15 years on corporate tax or Federal estate tax clients – avoid him or her.

IV.
Disaster Risks

There are two broad based disaster risks: natural and man-made. While terrorism is technically a man-made disaster risk, it merits its own discussion because the layer of protections is so unique. (See Exhibit #4, Severe Weather Warnings and Warnings Definitions).

A. Natural Disasters

Natural disasters are those largely created by mother nature. Floods, storms, earthquakes, etc. require many times that the Federal emergency authorities respond. So how can you protect your family against these emergencies? Let's review a few and other such disasters will carry much the same protections:

1. Flood: It is disturbing to note that most flood-related deaths can be avoided since most occur at night and are in automobiles. The following protections will help:

- Determine your flood risk: There are different reasons a community may flood including storm surge, river flooding, or heavy rainfall. Low-lying or poorly drained areas can also increase a community's flood risk. To protect yourself, learn what flood threats affect your community.

- Determine if there are rivers or creeks that flood frequently.

- Is your home located in a low-lying area?

- Determine your home's elevation.

- Have a flood preparation plan (See Exhibit 2 on designing a Family Disaster Plan).

- Determine whether you live in a potential flood zone.

- Keep abreast of road conditions through the news media. Move to a safe area before access is cut off by flood water.

- Develop a flood emergency action plan.

- Have flood insurance. Flood damage is not usually covered by home-owners insurance. Do not make assumptions. Check your policy.

- Buy flood insurance: There are times when you may be required to purchase flood insurance. If you buy a house in a designated high-risk area, and receive a mortgage loan from a federally regulated lender, your lender must, by law, require that you buy flood insurance. Coverage is available for residential and commercial buildings and contents, and can also be purchased by renters:

- Up to $250,000 for single-family, two-to-four family and other residential buildings.

- Up to $500,000 for non-residential buildings, including small business.

- Up to $100,000 for contents coverage for residences for owners and/or renters.

- Up to $500,000 for contents for businesses, including small businesses.

The National Flood Insurance Program is a pre-disaster flood mitigation and insurance protection program. The National Flood Insurance Program makes federally backed flood insurance available to residents and business owners. For more information   about the National Flood Insurance Program, call 1-888-CALL-FLOOD.

- Know your floods. Inland flooding is the leading weather-related cause of death in the United States. Every year, almost as many people die from flooding as from hurricanes, tornadoes and lightning combined. Most flood-related deaths and injuries could be avoided if people who come upon areas covered with water followed this simple advice: turn around, don't drown. Inland flooding usually occurs during or after a heavy, slow-moving rain storm. But it also can result from strong coastal storms. Severe inland flooding can occur in areas that are hundreds of miles from the eye of a hurricane.

Inland flooding that leads to drowning   usually occurs during flash-flood conditions.   Flash floods are those that develop within six hours of a rain storm. That may sound like a lot of time, but severe flash floods can occur   in a matter of minutes, depending on the intensity and duration of the rain, the topography of an area and the condition of the soil and ground cover. Nearly half of all flash-flood fatalities are vehicle-related. The majority of victims are males, but flood deaths affect people of both sexes and all age groups.

Anyone who has witnessed a flash flood can testify to the devastating power of fast-rushing water. Flash floods can roll boulders, uproot trees, destroy buildings and bridges, carry away vehicles and create deep new channels in the earth. Rapidly rising water can reach heights of 30 feet or more. Rain storms that trigger flash floods can also cause catastrophic mud slides.

2. Hurricane: Hurricanes, like tornadoes, can be downright life threatening. Here protection is essential – follow the guidelines below and you and your family should weather this force of nature.

- Know your hurricanes. Hurricanes are classified from category 1 to category 5 under the Saffir-Simpson Hurricane Intensity scale:

Category 1 – Winds 74-95 mph

- No real damage to building structures.

- Damage primarily to unanchored mobile homes, shrubbery and trees.

- Some coastal road flooding and minor pier damage.

Category 2 – Winds 96-110 mph

- Some roofing material, door and window damage to buildings.

- Considerable damage to vegetation, mobile homes and piers.

- Coastal and low-lying escape routes flood two to four hours before arrival of center.

- Small craft in unprotected anchorages break moorings.

Category 3 – Winds 111-130 mph

- Some structural damage to small residences and utility buildings with a minor account of curtain-wall failures.

- Mobile homes destroyed.

- Flooding near the coast destroys smaller structures with larger structures damages by floating debris.

- Terrain continuously lower than five feet above sea level may be flooded inland eight miles or more.

Category 4 – Winds 131-155 mph

- More extensive curtain wall failures with some complete roof structure failure on small residences.

- Major erosion on beach.

- Major damage to lower floors of structures near the shore.

- Terrain continuously lower than 10 feet above sea level may be flooded requiring massive evacuation of residential areas inland as far as six miles.

Category 5 – Winds greater than 155 mph

- Complete roof failure on many residences and industrial buildings.

- Some complete building failures with small utility buildings blown over or away.

- Major damage to lower floors of all structures located less than 15 feet above sea level and within 500 yards of the shoreline.

- Massive evacuation of residential areas on low ground within five to ten miles of the shoreline may be required.

- Always listen for warnings. Even though meteorologists have made improvements in the forecasting and tracking of severe weather, especially hurricanes, there is no way to predict in advance exactly how a storm will affect an area or when it will hit. This unpredictability makes "being alert" a vital factor in protecting homes, possessions and lives.

While trained officials and volunteers create a network to organize and oversee such things as evacuations and storm preparations, the responsibility for keeping in touch with changes in the threat lies with the public. By being aware and staying tuned to the local radio stations and television broadcasts, the general public is able to find out what to do, when to do it and where to go. Listen to the National Weather Service or NOAA broadcasting stations.

If a storm threatens, heed the advice from local authorities. Plan to evacuate early, and keep a full tank of gas during the hurricane season. Learn the best evacuation route before a storm forms and make arrangements with friends or relatives inland to stay with them until the storm has passed. Leave early, in daylight if possible, and never attempt to drive during a hurricane. After the storm, wait until the all-clear is given after the storm to return home. Avoid driving on coastal and low-lying roads because storm surge and hurricane-caused flooding are erratic and may occur with little or no warning.

- Insure and protect your property. Most homeowner policies will have a hurricane provision. Be certain the value of the damaged property is replacement value not original cost value.

- Move your most valuable possessions that you can't take with you to higher points within your home.

- Turn off gas, water, electricity. Check to see that you have done everything to protect your property from damage and loss.

- Lock windows and doors.

See the http://www.FEMA.gov. website.

- Never overlook pets. Decide on safe locations in your house where you could leave your pet in an emergency. (See Exhibit #3, Disaster Preparedness For Pets.)

- Consider easy to clean areas such as utility areas or bathrooms and rooms with access to a supply of fresh water.

- Avoid choosing rooms with hazards such as windows, hanging plants or pictures in large frames.

- In case of flooding, the location should have access to high counters that pets can escape to.

- Set up two separate locations if you have dogs and cats.

Buy a pet carrier that allows your pet to stand up and turn around inside. Train your pet to become comfortable with the carrier. Use a variety of training methods such as feeding it in the carrier or placing a favorite toy or blanket inside.

If your pet is on medication or a special diet, find out from your veterinarian what you should do in case you have to leave it alone for several days. Try and get an extra supply of medications.

Make sure your pet has a properly fitted collar that includes current license and rabies tag as well as an identification tag that has your name, address, and phone number.

If your dog normally wears a chain link "choker" collar, have a leather or nylon collar available if you have to leave him alone for several days. Keep your pet's shots current and know where the records are. Most kennels require proof of current rabies and distemper vaccinations before accepting a pet. Contact motels and hotels in communities outside of your area and find out if they will accept pets in an emergency.

When assembling emergency supplies for the household, include items for pets.

- Extra food (The food should be dry and relatively unappealing to prevent overeating. Store the foods in sturdy containers.)

- Kitty litter

- Large capacity self-feeder and water dispenser.

- Extra medications.

B. Man Made Disasters

These disasters are actually limited by the ingenuity – or depravity – of man. Heading the list are chemical (e.g. anthrax) and biological (e.g., viruses) risks to one's family.

Once again, after the risk and relative threat to you or your family is identified, the appropriate protection can be determined. The following illustrates the risk with a chemical disaster (anthrax) and what protections are deemed relevant.

- Know the nature of the man-made disaster: chemical or biological. Anthrax organisms can cause infection in the skin, gastrointestinal system or the lungs. To do so, the organism must be rubbed into abraded skin, swallowed or inhaled as a fine, aerosolized mist. The disease can be prevented after exposure to the anthrax spores by early treatment with the appropriate antibiotics. Anthrax is not spread from one person to another person.

For anthrax to be effective as a covert agent, it must be aerosolized into very small particles. This is difficult to do and requires a great deal of technical skill and special equipment. If those small particles are inhaled, a life-threatening lung infection can occur, but prompt recognition and treatment are effective.

- What protection is necessary, if suspected anthrax contamination?

- Remove heavily contaminated clothing as soon as possible and place in a plastic bag or some other container that can be sealed. This clothing should be given to the emergency responders for proper handling.

- Shower with soap and water as soon as possible. Do not use bleach or other disinfectant on your skin.

- Create, as with natural disasters, a disaster supplies kit. (See Exhibit #1, Family Disaster Supplies Kit.)

Pack essentials in a kit, e.g., medication, that can be transported to the place of evacuation. Have this kit prepared for each member of the family – including the household pet. See http://www.FEMA.Gov. See also http://RedCross.com.

V.
<u>Terrorism Risks</u>

A. <u>Nature of Risk</u>

The likelihood of you or your family experiencing a terrorist attack is very slight. However, it is this uncertainty that magnifies the risk. Being in the wrong place at the wrong time on 9-11 proved fatal to some. So how can you protect against it? The following entire section deals with this increasing reality of American life.

B. <u>How To Protect Against It</u>

The White House issued Homeland Security Directive 3 in March 2002 and established five threat conditions for possible terrorist attack. Across the country, questions like "What does a condition 'yellow' mean to my family?" are being asked. The American Red Cross has developed the following recommendations for the following areas for individuals and families.

AttackAction

Severe (Red)

- Complete recommended actions at lower levels.

- Listen to radio/TV for current information/instructions.

- Be alert to suspicious activity and report it to the proper authorities immediately.

- Contact business to determine status of work day.

- Adhere to any travel restrictions announced by local government authorities.

- Provide volunteer services only as requested.

- Discuss children's fears concerning possible/actual terrorist attacks.

High (Orange)

- Complete recommended actions at lower levels.

- Be alert to suspicious activity and report it to proper authorities.

- Review your personal and family disaster plans.

- Ensure communication plan is understood/practices by all family members.

- Exercise caution when traveling.

- Have shelter in place materials on hand and review procedure in Terrorism: Preparing for the Unexpected brochure.

- If a need is announced, donate blood at designated blood collection center.

- Prior to volunteering, contact agency to determine their needs.

- Discuss children's fears concerning possible/actual terrorist attacks.

Elevated (Yellow)

- Complete recommended actions at lower levels.

- Be alert to suspicious activity and report it to proper authorities.

- Ensure disaster supplies kit is stocked and ready.

- Check telephone numbers and email addresses in your personal communication plan and update as necessary.

- If not known to you, contact school to determine their emergency notification and evacuation plans for children.

- Develop alternate routes to/from work/school and practice them.

- Continue to provide volunteer services.

Guarded (Blue)

- Complete recommended actions at lower level.

- Be alert to suspicious activity and report it to proper authorities.

- Review stored disaster supplies and replace items that are outdated.

- Develop emergency communication plan with family/neighbors/friends.

- Establish an alternate meeting place away from home with family/friends.

- Provide volunteer services and take advantage of additional training opportunities.

Low (Green)

- Obtain copy of Terrorism: Preparing for the Unexpected Brochure from your local Red Cross chapter.

- Develop a personal disaster plan and disaster supplies kit (See Exhibits 1 and 2, Your Family Disaster Plan and Your Family Disaster Supplies Kit.)

- Examine volunteer opportunities in your community; choose an agency to volunteer with and receive initial training.

- T ake a Red Cross CPR/AED and first aid course.

- Always have a disaster plan. In my speeches around the country I'm always amazed at how few persons, even after 9-11, have a family or personal disaster plan. (See Exhibit 2, Family Disaster Plan.)

If this book does nothing else for you but cause you to develop a personal or family disaster plan, then it is worth it.

Unlike natural disasters where warnings precede the disaster in many cases, man- made disasters rely on the element of surprise or the lack of preparedness. Since your family is not together 24 hours a day, you need to consider how you would find each other in a disaster. Rally points (physical locations) should be identified for the most commonly frequented locations (i.e., work, school or neighbors). For example, if a crisis occurs at school – a location where both parents and child designate to meet should be included in your plan.

• Break the terrorist attack into components: before, during and after.

BEFORE

• Be alert and aware of your surroundings.

• Take precautions when traveling. Be aware of conspicuous or unusual behavior. Do not accept packages from strangers. Do not leave baggage unattended.

• Learn where emergency exits are located.

• Be ready to enact your Disaster Plan.

DURING

• Building Explosion – leave as quickly and calmly as possible.

• If items are falling from above – get under a sturdy table or desk.

• Fire – stay low to the floor and exit as quickly as possible. Cover your nose and mouth with a wet cloth. If a door is hot to the touch, do not open it – seek an alternate escape route. Stay below the smoke at all times.

AFTER

• If you are trapped in debris – use a flashlight. Cover your mouth with a piece of cloth. Tap on a pipe or wall so that rescuers can hear where you are. Use a whistle if available and shout as a last resort – shouting can result in inhalation of dangerous amounts of dust.

- Assisting victims – untrained persons should not attempt to rescue people in a collapsed building. Wait for emergency personnel to arrive.

- Chemical Agent – authorities will instruct you to either seek shelter and seal the premises or evacuate immediately. (See preceding section).

Addendum

This addendum is based solely on materials provided to the general public by the American Red Cross, the Federal Emergency Management Agency and the Humane Society of the United States. For further information consult the http://www.arc.org, http://www. FEMA.gov., http://www.HSUS.org. websites.

Exhibit 1:

Your Family Disaster Supplies Kit: Disasters happen anytime and anywhere. And when disaster strikes, you may not have much time to respond.

A highway spill of hazardous material could mean instant evacuation. A winter storm could confine your family at home. An earthquake, flood, tornado or any other disaster could cut off basic services – gas, water, electricity, and telephones – for days.

After a disaster, local officials and relief workers will be on the scene, but they cannot reach everyone immediately. You could get help in hours, or it may take days. Would your family be prepared to cope with the emergency until help arrives?

Your family will cope best by preparing for disaster before it strikes. One way to prepare is by assembling a Disaster Supplies Kit. Once disaster hits, you won't have time to shop or search for supplies. But if you've gathered supplies in advance, your family can endure an evacuation or home confinement.

To prepare your kit:

- Review the checklist in this exhibit.

- Gather the supplies that are listed. You may need them if your family is confined at home.

- Place the supplies you'd most likely need for an evacuation in an easy-to-carry container. These supplies are listed with an asterisk (*)

There are six basics you should stock in your home: water, food, first aid supplies, clothing and bedding, tools and emergency supplies and special items. Keep the items you would most likely need during an evacuation in a container such as a large, covered trash container, camping backpack, or a duffle bag.

Water: Store water in plastic containers such as soft drink bottles. Avoid using containers that will decompose or break, such as milk cartons or glass bottles. A normally active person needs to drink at least two quarts of water each day. Hot environments and intense physical activity can double that amount. Children, nursing mothers and ill people will need more.

Store one gallon of water per person per day (two quarts for drinking, two quarts for food preparation/sanitation)*

Keep at least a three-day supply of water for each person in your household.

Food: Store at least a three-day supply of non-perishable food. Select foods that require no refrigeration, preparation, or cooking and little or no water. If you must heat food, pack a can of sterno. Select food items that are compact and lightweight.

* Include a selection of the following foods in your Disaster Supplies Kit.

- Ready to eat canned meats, fruits, and vegetables.
- Canned juices, milk, soup (if powdered, store extra water).
- Staples – sugar, salt, pepper.
- High energy foods – peanut butter, jelly, crackers, granola bars, trail mix.
- Vitamins.
- Foods for infants, elderly persons or persons on special diets.
- Comfort/stress foods – cookies, hard candy, sweetened cereals, lollipops, instant coffee, tea bags.

First Aid Kit: Assemble a first aid kit for your home and one for each car. A first aid kit should include:

- Sterile adhesive bandages in assorted sizes.
- 2-inch sterile gauze pads (4-6)
- 4-inch sterile gauze pads (4-6)
- Hypoallergenic adhesive tape
- Triangular bandages (3)
- 2-inch sterile roller bandages (3 rolls)
- 3-inch sterile roller bandages (3 rolls)
- Scissors
- Tweezers
- Needle

- Moistened towelettes

- Antiseptic

- Thermometer

- Tongue blades (2)

- Tube of petroleum jelly or other lubricant

- Assorted sizes of safety pins

- Cleansing agent/soap

- Latex gloves (2 pair)

- Sunscreen

Nonprescription drugs

- Aspirin or non-aspirin pain reliever

- Anti-diarrhea medication

- Antacid (for stomach upset)

- Syrup of Ipecac (use to induce vomiting if advised by the Poison Control Center)

- Laxative

- Activated charcoal (use if advised by the Poison Control Center)

Tools and Supplies

- Mess kits, or paper cups, plates and plastic utensils *

- Emergency preparedness manual *

- Battery operated radio and extra batteries *

- Flashlight and extra batteries *

- Non-electric can opener, utility knife *

- Fire extinguisher: small canister, ABC type
- Tube tent
- Pliers
- Tape
- Compass
- Matches in a waterproof container
- Aluminum foil
- Plastic storage containers
- Signal flare
- Paper, pencil
- Needles, thread
- Medicine dropper
- Shut-off wrench, to turn off household gas and water
- Whistle
- Plastic sheeting
- Map of the area (for locating shelters)

Sanitation

- Toliet paper, towelettes *
- Soap, liquid detergent *
- Feminine supplies *
- Personal hygiene items *
- Plastic garbage bags, ties (for personal sanitation uses)
- Plastic bucket with tight lid
- Disinfectant
- Household chlorine bleach

Comfort and Bedding :

* Include at least one complete change of clothing and footwear per person.

- Study shoes or work boots *
- Rain gear *
- Blankets or sleeping bags *
- Hat and gloves
- Thermal underwear
- Sunglasses

Special Items: Remember family members with special needs, such as infants and elderly or disabled persons.

For Baby

- Formula
- Diapers
- Bottles
- Powdered milk
- Medications

For Adults

- Heart and high blood pressure medication
- Insulin

- Prescription drugs

- Denture needs

- Contact lenses and supplies

- Extra eye glasses

- Entertainment ,games and books

<u>Important Family Documents</u> – Keep these records in a waterproof portable container.

- Will, insurance policies, contracts, deeds, stocks and bonds

- Passports, social security cards, immunization records

- Bank account numbers

- Credit card account numbers and companies

- Inventory of valuable household goods, important telephone numbers

- Family records (birth, marriage, death certificates)

<u>Create a Family Disaster Plan:</u> To get started …
Contact your local emergency management or civil defense office and your local American Red Cross chapter.

- Find out which disasters are most likely to happen in your community.

- Ask how you would be warned.

- Find out how to prepare for each.

Meet with your family.

- Discuss the types of disasters that could occur.

- Explain how to prepare and respond.

- Discuss what to do if advised to evacuate.

- Practice what you have discussed.

Plan how your family will stay in contact if separated by disaster.

- Pick two meeting places: (1) a location a safe distance from your home in case of fire, (2) a place outside your neighborhood in case you can't return home.

- Choose an out-of-state friend as a "check-in contact" for everyone to call.

Complete these steps.

- Post emergency telephone numbers by every phone.

- Show responsible family members how and when to shut off water, gas and electricity at main switches.

- Install a smoke detector on each level of your home, especially near bedrooms; test monthly and change the batteries two times each year.

- Contact your local fire department to learn about home fire hazards.

- Learn first aid and CPR. Contact your local American Red Cross chapter for information and training.

Meet with your neighbors.

- Plan how the neighborhood could work together after a disaster.

- Know your neighbor's skills (medical, technical).

- Consider how you could help neighbors who have special needs, such as elderly or disabled persons.

- Make plans for child care in case parents can't get home.

Exhibit 2:

Family Disaster Plan: Where will your family be when disaster strikes? They could be anywhere... at work, at school, or in the car. How will you find each other? Will you know if your children are safe?

Disaster can strike quickly and without warning. It can force you to evacuate your neighborhood or confine you to your home. What would you do if basic services – water, gas, electricity or telephones -- were cut off? Local officials and relief workers will be on the scene after a disaster, but they cannot reach everyone right away.

Families can – and do – cope with disaster by preparing in advance and working together as a team. Follow the steps listed in this exhibit to create your family's disaster plan. Knowing what to do is your best protection and your responsibility.

Find Out What Could Happen To You: Contact your local emergency management or civil defense office and American Red Cross chapter – be prepared to take notes:

- Ask what types of disasters are most likely to happen. Request information on how to prepare for each.

- Learn about your community's warning signals: what they sound like and what you should do when you hear them.

- Ask about animal care after disaster. Animals may not be allowed inside emergency shelters due to health regulations.

- Find out how to help elderly or disabled persons, if needed.

- Next, find out about the disaster plans at your workplace, your children's school or daycare center and other places where your family spends time.

<u>Create A Disaster Plan:</u>   Meet with your family and discuss why you need to prepare for disaster. Explain the dangers of fire, severe weather and earthquakes to children. Plan to share responsibilities and work together as a team.

- Discuss the types of disasters that are most likely to happen. Explain what to do in each case.

- Pick two places to meet: (1) right outside the home in case of a sudden emergency, like a fire. (2) outside your neighborhood in case you can't return home. Everyone should know the address and phone number.

- Ask an out-of-state friend to be your "family contact". After a disaster, it's often easier to call long distance. Other family members should call this person and tell them where they are. Everyone must know your contact's phone number.

- Discuss what to do in an evacuation. Plan how to take care of your pets.

Complete this Checklist

- Post emergency telephone numbers by phones (fire, police, ambulance, etc.).

- Teach children how and when to call 911 or your local Emergency Medical Services number for emergency help.

- Show each family member how and when to turn off the water, gas, and electricity at the main switches.

- Check to see if you have adequate insurance coverage.

- Teach each family member how to use the fire extinguisher (ABC type), and show them where it's kept.

- Install smoke detectors on each level of your home, especially near bedrooms.

- Conduct a home hazard hunt.

- Stock emergency supplies and assemble a Disaster Supplies Kit.

- Take a Red Cross first aid and CPR class.

- Determine the best escape routes from your home. Find two ways out of each room.

- Find the safe spots in your home for each type of disaster.

Practice and Maintain Your Plan

- Quiz your kids every six months so they remember what to do.

- Conduct fire and emergency evacuation drills.

- Replace stored water every three months and stored food every six months.

- Test and recharge your fire extinguisher(s) according to manufacturer's instructions.

- Test your smoke detectors monthly and change the batteries at least once a year.

Exhibit 3:

Disaster Preparedness For Pets: When disaster strikes, always keep your pets with you. If it isn't safe for you to stay put, it isn't safe for your pets.

Hurricanes, floods, wildfires, hazardous material spills – disasters can strike anytime, anywhere. If you think you will never have to evacuate unless you live in a flood plain, near an earthquake fault line or in a coastal area, you may be tragically mistaken. It is imperative that you make preparations to evacuate your family and your pets in any situation. In the event of a disaster, proper preparation will play off with the safety of your family and pets.

If You Evacuate, Take Your Pets: The single most important thing you can do to protect your pets is to take them with you when you evacuate. Animals left behind can easily be injured, lost, or killed. Animals left inside your home can escape through storm-damaged areas, such as broken windows. Animals turned loose to fend for themselves are likely to become victims to exposure, starvation, predators, contaminated food or water, or accidents. Leaving dogs tied or chained outside in a disaster is a death sentence.

- If you leave, even if you think you may be gone only for a few hours, take your animals. Once you leave, you have no way of knowing how long you'll be kept out of the area, and you may not be able to go back for your pets.

- Leave early – don't wait for a mandatory evacuation order. An unnecessary trip is far better than waiting too long to leave safely with your pets. If you wait to be evacuated by emergency officials, you may be told to leave your pets behind.

Don't Forget ID: Your pets should be wearing up-to-date identification at all times. It's a good idea to include the phone number of a friend or relative outside your immediate area – if your pet is lost, you'll want to provide a number on the tag that will be answered even if you're out of your home.

Find a Safe Place Ahead of Time: Because evacuation shelters generally don't accept pets (except for service animals) you must plan ahead to ensure that your family and pets will have a safe place to stay. Don't wait until disaster strikes to do your research.

- Contact hotels and motels outside your immediate area to check policies on accepting pets. Ask about any restrictions on number, size, and species. Ask if "no pet" policies would be waived in an emergency. Make a list of pet-friendly places and keep it handy. Call ahead for a reservation as soon as you think you might have to leave your home.

- Check with friends, relatives, or others outside your immediate area. Ask if they would be able to shelter you and your animals or just your animals, if necessary. If you have more than one pet, you may have to be prepared to house them separately.

- Make a list of boarding facilities and veterinary offices that might be able to shelter animals in emergencies; include 24-hour telephone numbers.

- Ask your local animal shelter if it provides foster care or shelter for pets in an emergency. This should be your last resort, as shelters have limited resources and are likely to be stretched to their limits during an emergency.

If You Don't Evacuate: If your family and pets wait out a storm or other disaster at home, identify a safe area of your home where you can all stay together.

- Keep dogs on leashes and cats in carriers, and make sure they are wearing identification.

- Have any medications and a supply of pet food and water inside watertight containers, along with your other emergency supplies.

As The Disaster Approaches: Don't wait until the last minute to get ready. Warnings of hurricanes or other disasters may be issued hours, or even days, in advance.

- Call to confirm emergency shelter arrangements for you and your pets.

- Bring pets into the house and confine them so you can leave with them quickly if necessary. Make sure each pet and pet carrier has up-to-date identification and contact information. Include information about your temporary shelter location.

- Make sure your disaster supplies are ready to go, including your pet disaster kit.

In Case You're Not Home: An evacuation order may come, or a disaster may strike, when you're at work or out of the house.

- Make arrangements well in advance for a trusted neighbor to take your pets and meet you at a specified location. Be sure the person is comfortable with your pets, knows where your animals are likely to be, knows where your disaster supplies are kept, and has a key to your home.

- If you use a pet sitting service, it may be able to help, but discuss the possibility well in advance.

After the Storm: Planning and preparation will help you weather the disaster, but your home may be a very different place afterward, whether you have taken shelter at home or elsewhere.

- Don't allow your pets to roam loose. Familiar landmarks and smells might be gone, and your pet will probably be disoriented. Pets can easily get lost in such situations.

- For a few days, keep dogs on leashes and keep cats in carriers inside the house. If your house is damaged, they could escape and become lost.

- Be patient with your pets after a disaster. Try to get them back into their normal routines as soon as possible, and be ready for behavioral problems that may result from the stress of the situation. If behavioral problems persist, or if your pet seems to having any health problems, talk to your veterinarian.

Evacuation Planning: You may not be in a flood zone or have to flee wildfire, but even a hazardous material incident on a nearby street could force you to evacuate. It pays to be prepared!

Disaster Supply Checklist for Pets: Every member of your family should know what he or she needs to take when you evacuate. You also need to prepare supplies for your pet. Stock up on non-perishables well ahead of time, add perishable items at the last minute, and have everything ready to go at a moment's notice. Keep everything accessible, stored in sturdy containers (duffel bags, covered trash containers, etc.) that can be carried easily.

In your disaster kit, you should include:

- Medications and medical records stored in a waterproof container and a first aid kit. A pet first aid book is also good to include.

- Sturdy leashes, harnesses, and carriers to transport pets safely and to ensure that your pets can't escape. Carriers should be large enough for the animal to stand comfortably, turn around, and lie down. Your pet may have to stay in the carrier for hours at time while you have taken shelter away from home. Be sure to have a secure cage with no loose objects inside it to accommodate smaller pets. These may require blankets or towels for bedding and warmth, and other special items.

- Current photos and descriptions of your pets to help others identify them in case you and your pets become separated and to prove that they are yours.

- Food and water for at least three days for each pet, bowls, cat litter, and litter box, and a manual can opener.

- Information on feeding schedules, medical conditions, behavior problems, and the name and number of your veterinarian in case you have to board your pets or place them in foster care.

- Pet beds and toys, if you can easily take them, to reduce stress.

Other useful items include newspapers, paper towels, plastic trash bags, grooming items, and household bleach.

Other Evacuation Tips

- All mobile home residents should evacuate at the first sign of a disaster.

- Evacuate to the safest location you can find that's as close as possible to home. Long-distance evacuation can be a problem when highways are crowded.

- When planning for hurricanes, identify your evacuation zone and level to determine if and when you would have to evacuate. Be prepared for one category higher than the one forecast, because hurricanes often increase in strength just before making landfall.

- Y our local humane organization or local emergency management agency may be able to provide you with information about your community's disaster response plans.

Exhibit 4:

Severe Weather Watches and Warnings Definitions

Flood Watch: Flooding conditions are actually occurring or are imminent in the warning.

Flood Warning: Flash flooding is possible in or close to the watch area. Flash floods are generally issued for flooding that is expected to occur within 6 hours after heavy rains ended.

Flash Flood Warning: Flash flooding is actually occurring or imminent in the warning area issued as a result of torrential rains, a dam failure, or ice jam.

Tornado Watch: Conditions are conducive to the development of tornadoes in and close to the area.

Tornado Warning: A tornado has actually been sighted by spotters or indicated on radar occurring or imminent in the warning area.

Severe Thunderstorm Watch: Conditions are conducive to the development of severe thunderstorms in and close to the watch area.

Severe Thunderstorm Warning: A severe thunderstorm has actually been observed on radar, and is occurring or imminent in the warning area.

Tropical Storm Watch: Tropical storm conditions with sustained winds from 39 to 73 mph possible in the watch area within the next 36 hours.

Tropical Storm Warning: Tropical storm conditions are expected in the warning area within 24 hours.

Hurricane Watch: Hurricane conditions (sustained winds greater than 73 mph) are possible in the watch area within 36 hours.

Hurricane Warning: Hurricane conditions are expected in the warning area within 24 hours.

About the Author

Harold S. Peckron is a nationally recognized expert on the Alternative Minimum Tax. In addition to writing on the subject, he has taught tax as a tenured law professor and as a seminar leader to professional groups. He has served in government and private industry and his tax career spans over three decades.

Harold holds several graduate degrees including an L.L.M. in Taxation from the Georgetown University of Law School. His interests include running marathons and writing. He lives in Florida.